NORTHUMBERLAND
SCHOOLS LIBRARY SERVICE

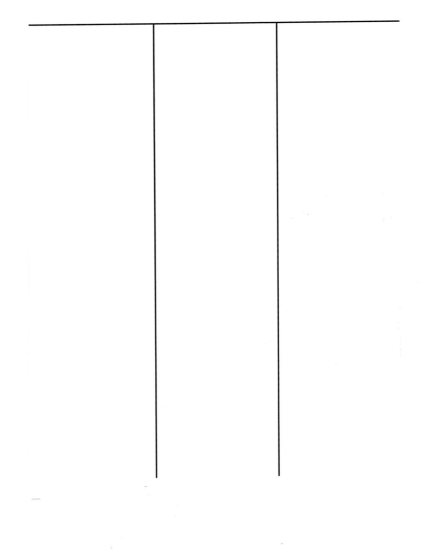

AMPHIBIANS

by
Charlie Ogden

©2017
Book Life
King's Lynn
Norfolk PE30 4LS

ISBN: 978-1-78637-100-3

A catalogue record for this book
is available from the British Library.

Written by:
Charlie Ogden

Edited by:
Grace Jones

Designed by:
Danielle Jones

CONTENTS

Words that are <u>underlined</u> are explained in the glossary on page 31.

THE ANIMAL KINGDOM

The animal kingdom includes over 8 million known living <u>species</u>. They come in many different shapes and sizes, they each do weird and wonderful things and they live all over planet Earth.

From the freezing Arctic waters to the hottest desert in the world, animals have <u>adapted</u> to the often extreme and diverse conditions upon Earth.

Even though each and every species of animal is <u>unique</u>, they still share certain characteristics with each other. These shared characteristics are used to classify animals. There are six main groups used to classify animals. They are; mammals, reptiles, birds, insects, amphibians and fish.

10,000 new species of animal are discovered every year.

Amphibians include frogs, toads, salamanders and newts.

AMPHIBIANS

WHAT IS AN AMPHIBIAN?

An amphibian is a type of animal that lays eggs, has a backbone and has a thin, moist, <u>permeable</u> skin.

All amphibians are amphibious, which means that they can live on land and in water. Amphibians are also cold-blooded animals, which means that their body temperatures change with the temperature of their environments.

Frogs are amphibians who lay their eggs, called frogspawn, in fresh water.

There are around 7,000 known species of amphibian alive today. They come in many different shapes and sizes and they all have their own individual features that help them to survive in their habitats. Salamanders, newts, frogs and toads are all types of amphibian.

Chinese Giant Salamander

Paedophyrne Amauensis

The largest amphibian on Earth is the Chinese giant salamander, which is around 1.8 metres long, whilst a frog species called paedophyrne amauensis is the smallest amphibian – and vertebrate – on Earth measuring in at just 0.7 centimetres long.

AMPHIBIAN CHECKLIST

- Lays eggs
- Lives in water and on land
- Thin, moist, permeable skin
- Cold-blooded
- Vertebrate

BODY PARTS

Even though amphibians can look very different from one another, there are certain <u>traits</u> that nearly all species of amphibian share.

People use these traits to group amphibians together and to work out whether an animal is an amphibian or not. One of the main ways that amphibians are grouped together is through their ability to live both on land and in water.

However, amphibians also share many similarities in the parts of their bodies. For example, all amphibians are vertebrates, meaning that they have backbones, and they are all cold-blooded.

Red-eyed Tree Frog

Fire Salamander

Caecilian

Amphibians come in lots of different shapes, sizes and colours.

SKIN

Amphibians have unique skins that help them to survive. An amphibian's skin will usually be permeable, very soft and covered in a thin layer of slime that helps to keep it moist. As well as this, many species of amphibian are able to breathe through their skin both when they are underwater and when they are on land. Because the skins of amphibians are so special, people can use them to identify whether an animal is an amphibian or not.

Some frogs also have very brightly coloured skin, which shows other animals that they are poisonous and dangerous to eat.

Poison Dart Frog

AMPHIBIAN ORDERS

All the different classes of animal, such as reptiles, mammals and amphibians, can be broken down into smaller groups called orders.

Most classes of animal are made up of lots of different orders but the class of amphibians is only split into three orders: Anura, Caudata and Gymnophiona.

The order Anura is the largest amphibian order and it is made up of frogs and toads. Most of the species in this order have long back legs, <u>webbed toes</u>, large eyes and long, sticky tongues that are used to catch insects. Most male frogs also have one or two vocal sacs, which are thin flexible patches of skin found under their mouths that they can inflate in order to attract females.

A male frog inflating its vocal sac.

Frogs have very **smooth** skins whereas **toads** have **bumpy** skins with lots of **warts.**

Can you tell which is the toad and which is the frog?

The order Caudata is made up of amphibians that look similar to lizards, such as salamanders and newts. Although these animals look similar to lizards, which are reptiles, they are still amphibians as they have a smooth, slimy skin instead of <u>scales</u>. Animals in this order usually have tails, short legs and long, thin bodies.

Smooth and slimy skin

Scales

Eastern Red-spotted Newt

The final order of amphibians – Gymnophiona – is made up of a weird group of animals that look a lot like worms. These animals, known as caecilians, usually have very small eyes and very bad eyesight compared to other amphibians. This is because caecilians mostly live underground, where it is too dark to see anything – no matter how good your eyes are!

Caecilian

GETTING AROUND

Frogs are known for being some of the best jumpers in the animal kingdom.

Their long and strong back legs mean that they can push off from the ground with lots of power. While in the air, frogs hold their front legs close to their chest and leave their back legs extended behind them, as this is the most <u>streamline</u> position. Frogs' long back legs and webbed toes also make them very good swimmers.

Relative to their **size**, **frogs** are the best **jumpers** out of all of the vertebrates.

Malagasy Rainbow Frog

There are some frog species that are able to get around in ways other than jumping and swimming. The Malagasy rainbow frog uses its powerful legs and strong claws in order to climb walls. It is the only rock-climbing frog in the world!

BREATHING

Like all animals, amphibians need to breathe and most adult amphibians breathe in a very special way – through their skin. These amphibians are able to exchange <u>gases</u> in their bodies through their skin with <u>oxygen</u> in the air or in water. In order to be able to exchange gases through their skin fast enough, amphibians need to keep their skin soft and moist.

While most amphibians are able to breathe through their skin, many species still have organs called <u>lungs</u> in order to breathe the air. As well as this, lots of young amphibians have organs called <u>gills</u> that allow them to breathe underwater.

PREDATORS AND PREY

All animals can be sorted into groups depending on what they eat. The three groups are carnivores, herbivores and omnivores.

Herbivores
Plant-eaters

Carnivores
Meat-eaters

Omnivores
Plant and meat-eaters

Brazilian Tree Frog

African Bullfrog

Nearly all amphibians are carnivores, feeding mostly on beetles, caterpillars, worms and spiders as these animals are slow and easy to catch. However, there are some exceptions. The huge African bullfrog eats almost any animal that it comes across, even birds, and the Brazilian tree frog eats lots of fruit as well as insects, making it an omnivore.

Animals that hunt other animals are called predators, whereas animals that are hunted by other animals are called prey.

Unlike other groups of animal, nearly all amphibians are both predators and prey. This is because they are bigger than most insects, which are often their prey, but are usually small enough to be eaten by larger animals, such as birds, foxes and snakes.

A big-eyed tree frog trying to catch a fly with its tongue.

However, there are some amphibians that aren't hunted by any predators. Chinese giant salamanders are very big and they mostly live near small, muddy streams that are far away from other large animals. Because of this, they do not have any natural predators in the wild.

Chinese Giant Salamander

FORESTS, PONDS AND STREAMS

For many species of amphibian, it is essential that they live in a habitat that is in or near to a pond or a stream.

This is because it is important that their skin does not dry out. As well as this, most amphibian young need to spend the first part of their lives underwater.

Two frogs in a pond.

Ponds are a great place to find frogs, toads and newts. If you have a pond near to where you live, why not go and see what amphibians you can find there!

The three species of giant salamander, which are the Chinese giant salamander, the Japanese giant salamander and the hellbender salamande all prefer to live in fast-flowing water, such as streams and rivers.

A Japanese giant salamander underwater.

One third of all **salamander** species are <u>native</u> to **North America.**

There are species of frog that live in forest habitats, even though water can be hard to find. These frogs are often called tree frogs as many of them spend their lives in trees.

A **group** of **frogs** is called an 'army'.

Some tree frogs have developed amazing ways to deal with the lack of water in their habitats. The red-eyed tree frog lays its eggs on a leaf above a puddle and produces a special jelly to keep the eggs moist until they hatch. It would be too dangerous to leave the eggs in the puddle as it could dry out and a predator could find them. When the eggs hatch, the young fall into the puddle and begin their lives.

The frogspawn of a red-eyed tree frog stuck to a leaf.

ADAPTATION

Amphibians have adapted to their environments in many amazing ways.

Adaptations often help an animal to survive in extreme habitats or ward-off predators and amphibians provide some of the best examples of adaptation in the entire animal kingdom. Newts, as well as some salamanders, are able to regrow large parts of their bodies in a process called regeneration. Newts are able to regrow their legs, their eyes and even their hearts! This unique adaptation is very useful in the wild, as it means that a newt that has been injured by a predator is more likely to survive.

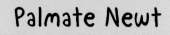

Palmate Newt

While most amphibians live in or near to water, there are some species that live in deserts. These amphibians have had to adapt in order to be able to survive these dry habitats. One amphibian that lives in a desert habitat is the spadefoot toad. This toad survives in the desert by burrowing into the ground using hardened areas on its back legs called spades. These burrows keep the toad cool and stop it from drying out when the temperature becomes too hot. They also provide safety and shelter from desert predators, such as eagles and vultures.

Spadefoot toads dig backwards into the ground and enter their burrows back-legs first.

A spadefoot toad poking its head out of its burrow.

LIFE CYCLES

The life cycle of an animal is the series of changes that it goes through from the start to the end of its life.

Amphibians have some of the most exciting life cycles out of all of the animals in the animal kingdom, as most species go through a transformation known as a metamorphosis. Most amphibians have to lay their eggs in water as amphibian young cannot live on land like the adults can. Before they undergo the metamorphosis, amphibian young are said to be in the larval stage of their life. Amphibians in the larval stage look very different to adults of their species and won't begin to look like adults until after their metamorphoses.

These are tadpoles, which is what we call frogs that are in the larval stage of their life.

Possibly the most important part of the life cycle is the reproduction process, which involves finding a mate, the <u>fertilisation</u> of eggs and the production of young. It is more difficult for female salamanders to find a mate than it is for most animals because male and female salamanders often look the same. Because of this, female salamanders have to use their sense of smell to find a mate. There is a lot of variation between salamanders when it comes tolaying eggs. Some species of salamander lay lots of eggs in order to increase the chance that some will survive, whereas other salamander mothers will lay only a few eggs in a well-hidden spot and then protect them from predators until they hatch.

This female fire salamander is ready to lay her eggs in the water.

LIFE CYCLE OF A FROG

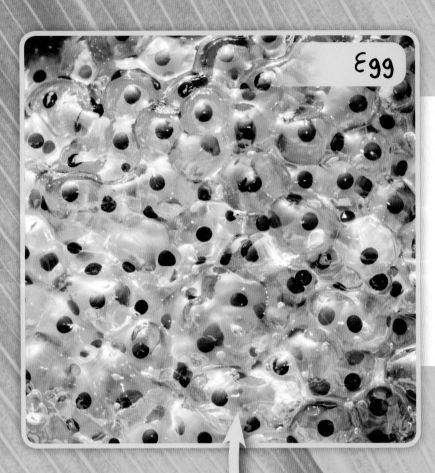

Egg

A female frog lays her eggs in still, fresh water. A frog's eggs are called frogspawn and they stick together in large groups as this helps to protect them from predators.

The froglet continues to grow bigger and it will eventually lose its tail altogether. Once this has happened, the metamorphosis is complete and the tadpole has become a fully grown adult. The adult frog will now begin to look for a mate in order to start the reproduction process again.

Adulthood

Tadpole

The tiny black dot in each egg develops into a tadpole over the next few weeks. Each tadpole has a tail that helps it to wriggle out of its egg and swim around, as well as a set of gills that allow it to breathe underwater.

Froglet

The tadpole spends a few weeks eating as much food as it can. After it has eaten enough food, the tadpole begins its metamorphosis. It grows two back legs and then two front legs, all while its tail becomes shorter. The tadpole also grows a pair of lungs that allow it to breathe air at the surface of the water. Once this has happened, the tadpole has become a froglet.

AMPHIBIANS

Some amphibians have developed extreme habits or skills that help them to survive.

One such extreme amphibian is the long-nosed horned frog. This very unique looking frog species has developed large, horn-shaped pieces of skin above its eyes and snout. As well as this, the long-nosed horned frog also has folds in the skin on its back and sides. The unusual look of this frog helps it to blend in with leaves and sticks on the forest floor. This allows the long-nosed horned frog to wait, hidden amongst the leaves, until a spider or lizard moves close enough to grab!

LONG-NOSED HORNED FROG

Size:
10 – 12 cm long

Home:
Rainforests in Southeast Asia

Diet:
Spiders, lizards, mice and other frogs

Long-nosed Horned Frog

GLASS FROG

The glass frog of Central and South America has skin that is so thin that parts of it, especially on its <u>abdomen</u>, are transparent. This means that you can see through it! These tiny frogs spend a lot of their time in trees trying to stay hidden from predators. Because of this, scientists believe that the glass frog's transparent skin may help them to blend in with their environment and escape being eaten by larger animals. However, all we know for certain is that this is one of the most unusual amphibians on the planet.

Size:
3 – 7.5 cm long

Home:
Forests in Central and South America

Diet:
Spiders and insects

A glass frog showing off its transparent skin.

CAECILIAN

Caecilians have developed a way of feeding their young that is completely unique within the animal kingdom. The caecilian mother develops a thick outer skin that is high in fat and other <u>nutrients</u>. Once she has done this, her young start to peel off her skin and eat it using their sharp, claw-like teeth. While feeding off of their mother's skin, caecilian young are able to grow by up to ten times their own weight in just a week! Don't worry about the mother though – she is able to regrow her skin as fast as her young eat it and it doesn't seem to cause her any pain.

A caecilian mother with her eggs.

Size:
Up to 1.5 m long

Home:
Underground in wet areas of Central America, South America, West Africa, India and Southeast Asia

Diet:
Worms and insects

MEXICAN SALAMANDER

There are some salamander species that don't go through metamorphosis or develop lungs after the larval stage of their life, instead staying underwater for their entire lives and breathing using gills. However, unlike most animals that breathe using gills, salamander young have their gills on the outside of their bodies. These are called external gills. This means that all the species of salamander that don't go through metamorphosis still have gills on the outside of their bodies when they are adults!

One species of salamander that does this is the axolotl, or the Mexican salamander, and many people think that their gills make them look cute.

Size: 23 – 30 cm long
Home: Lake Xochimilco in Mexico
Diet: Worms, insects and small fish

An axolotl showing off its external gills.

AMPHIBIANS UNDER THREAT

Many species of amphibian are in danger of becoming <u>extinct</u>. One problem facing these animals is <u>pollution</u>.

Rubbish, plastic and chemicals are being dumped in many different habitats around the world, especially the lakes, ponds, rivers and streams that many amphibians need in order to survive. Unless serious action is taken soon, many species of amphibian could become extinct because they cannot find clean and safe water in which to lay their eggs.

The axolotl is now only native to one lake in Mexico, as its other natural habitats have been destroyed by humans. This final lake is very small and many scientists fear that there wil soon be no axolotls left in the wild.

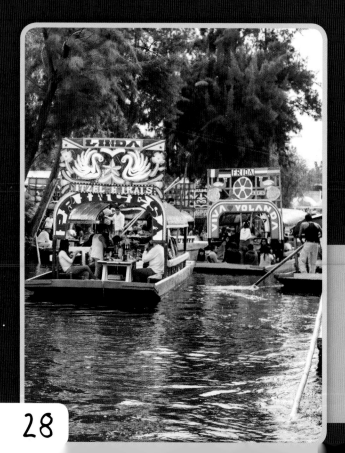

Lake Xochimilco, the last natural home of axolotls, is used by people for lots of different reasons, many of which add to the pollution in the lake.

Another problem facing amphibians today is habitat destruction. One way that humans destroy habitats is through the cutting down of forests in order to collect wood, which is known as deforestation. The Amazon rainforest in South America is being destroyed through deforestation. In the last 40 years, an area of the Amazon rainforest the size of France has been destroyed through deforestation. This has already caused species of amphibians to die out and, if it continues, it is likely that many more species will also become extinct.

There are hundreds, maybe thousands, of species of amphibian in the Amazon rainforest that need to be protected from deforestation.

Huge areas of the Amazon rainforest are destroyed every day.

FIND OUT MORE

BOOKS

Amphibians (Living Things & Their Habitats) by Grace Jones

(BookLife, 2016)

Animal Classification (Discover & Learn) by Steffi Cavell-Clarke

(BookLife, 2017)

WEBSITES

WWF
www.wwf.org.uk

On this website you can follow links to information on all sorts of endangered animals and find out what WWF is doing to save wildlife.

BBC NATURE
www.bbc.co.uk/nature/life/Amphibian/by/rank/all

Learn about different species of amphibian and their habitats.

GLOSSARY

abdomen	the part of the body that contains the reproductive and digestive organs
adapted	changed over time to suit an environment
extinct	a species of animal that no longer exists
fertilisation	the process of causing an egg to develop into a new living thing
gases	air-like substances that fill any space available
gills	the organs that some animals use to breathe underwater
habitats	the natural homes or environments of living things
lungs	the organs that allow some animals to breathe air
metamorphosis	the transformation that the young of some species must go through in order to become adults
native	originally from
nutrients	substances that plants and animals need in order to grow and survive
oxygen	a gas that all living things need to breathe in order to stay alive
permeable	something that allows liquid or gas to pass through it
pollution	the introduction of a substance into an environment that has harmful effects
scales	the thin, bony plates that protect the skin of fish and reptiles
species	a group of very similar animals that are capable of producing young together
streamline	the position that creates the least resistance to water or air
traits	qualities or characteristics
unique	unlike anything else
webbed toes	toes that have a thin layer of skin stretching between them
vertebrate	an animal with a backbone

INDEX